We Come Elemental

TAMIKO BEYER

ALICE JAMES BOOKS

FARMINGTON, MAINE

© 2013 by Tamiko Beyer
All rights reserved
Printed in the United States

10 9 8 7 6 5 4 3 2 1

Alice James Books are published by Alice James Poetry Cooperative, Inc., an affiliate of the University of
Maine at Farmington.

Alice James Books
238 Main Street
Farmington, ME 04938
www.alicejamesbooks.org

Library of Congress Cataloging-in-Publication Data

Beyer, Tamiko.
  We come elemental / Tamiko Beyer.
     pages cm
  ISBN 978-1-938584-00-8 (pbk. : alk. paper)
  I. Title.
  PS3602.E936W4 2013
  811'.6--dc23
                          2012047351

Alice James Books gratefully acknowledges support from individual donors, private foundations, the
University of Maine at Farmington, and the National Endowment for the Arts.

ART WORKS.
arts.gov

Cover Photograph of Antony Gormley's sculpture "Another Place": "Another Place, Crosby Beach,
Merseyside", Ian Britton.

Table of Contents

Acknowledgments

My heart is full of thanks for all who have helped bring this book into its present manifestation.

Many thanks to all my teachers and peers, and to the communities of poets and activists I have been privileged to be a part of. In particular, I am grateful to my dear friends and mentors in Kundiman and to my queer Agent 409 family. I am lucky to travel on this fierce, difficult, and gorgeous path with you.

Deep gratitude to all the creatures and beings of the water and the earth, and to the ancestors and the spirits of the land, sky, and sea.

Always, love to my family: Mom, Dad, Michael, Matthew, Mocean, and Kian.

Finally, grateful acknowledgment to the editors of the following journals and anthologies in which the following poems first appeared, often in different versions:

A Joint Called Pauline
Another & Another: An Anthology from the Grind Daily Writing Series
Anti-
Bone Bouquet
DIAGRAM

Esque

H_NGM_N

Lantern Review

Little Red Leaves

Locuspoint: New York City

No Tell Motel

Octopus

Poemeleon

Poets for Living Waters

South Dakota Review

Spoon River Poetry Review

Sweet

Quarterly West

For Kian, my heart and my life.

And for the disappearing, and the disappeared.

It is hard to turn away from moving water.

—Lyn Hejinian

Given the chance, what disappears will one day
come home again.

—Gwen Thompkins

BODY GEOGRAPHIES

Look Alive, Dark Side

Since our boat days
we've trusted
the stars' chart –
each season's sky.
Now we climb. Stone as cold
as metal rivets. We do not know how
we will die, but we will die.
In space, all machinery
floats away.

—

Blue flash, quick skate
through atmosphere. *This is not
your father's moon* –

dead drought, tattered flag litter. What's the point
of the horizon line if not for demarcation?
This side: well. To drink, to breathe, to fuel. That side: debris.

Home, we watch the pale coin of midnight rise.
Our mouths slick with desire, measuring tools ready at the ready.
Nothing like a tall glass of mooncold.

———

Beach walking we
who siphon the wet
step around dumb
lumps gleaming
in moonlight's pull:
creatures the tide
abandons to the shore.
We are not at all like them.

Disorient

What light there is –
wave, a gentle movement.

We enter the space without walls,
without windows, but with a roof.

⁓

We are remembering what arrival feels like in the narrows.
We are remembering to breathe if little else.

We were the fattened when the future
found itself shut up among the penury.

⁓

A lie as flawless as water
when it shines under the late moon. But even then

we find each other – muted bodies a call across land, across sea.
Anemone, kelp. Hermit crab, a swift presentation of injury.

Keep home on the mind. Fight the body
ensconced in a whorl of calcium carbonate.

The biggest wins, the meanest, the trickiest, the most relentless.
All the minerals boil down to an empty grid. We who will not be
    contained.

Water West

Diablo

I'm wild all the way up the craggy Cascades, feral girl in a dented station wagon chugging over Highway 20. The pass twists, stone face rises, pines spear the glint sky. I'm looking for the dam and its lake – there, there – round the bend: pure turquoise squared off and deep as sky's deep. Devil blue water I want to dip my blister body into, my ragged skin into your perfect wet. Your cool, captured absence – no mud, no algae, all angled. How does water do that? I stop for gas and think what it'd be like to live in this little grid town built by the electric company along with the turbines and power lines, a life accompanied by electromagnetic spin. Every day clock in and run lights down the mountain to the city, clock out and watch the stars come out in the thin night sky.

Concrete slab, you dam –
I charge the water-rush, arc
ions lusting loose.

SF Fog

When water splits land we want a crossing. All the ways we
lose ourselves. Red-orange bridge spans constant, the arc's cut
under morning sun. But it dims in the fog rolling up thick from
the Pacific. Cold particles cling to skin, enter lungs – water
breaching air, no use for solid shore. It rolls into the city, seeps
over steep streets. I want to find home; I start under the wet
rainbow. Then move past the white bank resting against Mt.
Sutro's flank, move into the sunshine, into the patio full of
women dancing with each other under lemon trees. Stay long
enough for the one with curls to whisper in my ear. The Bay's
mythology: how a whale once entered from the ocean, then
found her way out again, swallowing the sun.

I refuse landing:
many parts this and many parts that –
only water mine.

Lake Merritt

Night in Oakland and an echoed suggestion of stars: my
footsteps under the lake's strung necklace of lights. Stop to
watch a snowy egret fish at the flood-control gates where
lake roils through in search of bay. Uplit, the bird's feathers
glow orange, its neck an elegant *S*, its black beak dipping into
spume – all plankton and wriggling fish. Bird and girl at the
banks of a body rich in molecular history: once estuary, once
Ohlone hunting ground, once sewer full of ammonia runoff from
gold boomtown. Now lake of nightwalks for us in search of
geographic instruction.

We do alter, we
do deny. I wait too
in the wet wake.

Compass

Cohesion of asphalt might be a straight shot
but the relic channel brings us closer
to water's residue. Keep in earshot of the metal-grey river,

our bodies split through by the meridian.
When we unloose the latitudes
we feel as if we are dying but we will not die.

The journey is several days or several years –
depends on how we undo the doing.
Replenish at the creek, upstream, where clear

means clear, where melt stings cold.
Fork left at the stand of blighted trees.
There are only some ways to outsmart the body.

No time left for sleep, though we may
reinvent the meaning of sleep.
We cannot predict the calling

that will pulse through our capillaries,
the cardinal points tapping
their imperatives against our skeleton's scaffold.

When we encounter topography's wild,
we'll feel our edges blur. We'll give in
to the river's fold until horizon loses definition.

Due north then due east –
all we've packed into the suitcase becomes
as heavy as water to abandon.

We've set the center askew.
When we can no longer lift the stunning map.
When we no longer need permission.

We Come Elemental

We step into humid light.
It sticks to our skin
and microbes gorge
in greywater runoff pools.

The chlorophyll chorus sings
our collected chemical stew –
nitrogen! nitrogen! nitrogen!

      Each molecule polished
      each **o** each pair of **h** a banquet of lust –

            wet sludge::
            stream suds::
            oil slick rain::

            ::eat the bread of our body's slough
            ::eat our bread the crumbed down drain
            ::eat of our bread our rainbowed fuel

until clear pools
flow back to the rivers
– those quick veins of industry –

wash over ancient mollusk shells

and we learn again
green's good
was light veined
through leaves.

Trash Sail

terrafirma

        tip of tongue
        behind the teeth

us

wash   break beat   break water   break tide
wash flotsam   wash plummet

      wash all we
      all defined

unsinkable

trawling boats haul up netfuls
oceantrash translucent
every little piece of plastic manufactured
fifty years floating   still
here: North Pacific Gyre
confetti-dense   suspended vortex
invisible to satellites

matter

salt   fresh

one bag

      two soles

            three net

                four beer

                    five cond

                        six cre

                            seven bo

                                eight l

                                  nine

                                    te

andso   andso

      gyre

plstcplstcplsticplsticplsticplstisplstic

(weather)   we   raft

      typhoon   or   hurricane

salt   fresh

bent   sun

layer   turtle   feed

seagull   sea   welt

knot   flash   day   fish

kiss   star   lash

polymer

we   balloon

creature

tontross	fishplank	jellyalba
planktross	jellyton	albafish
trossjelly	tonfish	plankalba

rise

so sail the horse latitudes
so sail a week through stew
nurdles   lego block   toothbrush
lighter   jewel case   traffic cone
rope coil uncoiled at length
so sail and sail and sail and sail and sail
and sail and sail and sail and sail and sail

Wade

Because no disaster is perfect
there are mistakes made
made in every single disaster
because

In the diffuse
light
after
the rain
dawn becomes
a hesitant
mirror
because

     We
     in an attic
     watch
     the slow rise
         water thick
     inside and out

16

become a drenched
                mouth
     that envelops
     because

I received conflicting information
I received information
approximately
the levees had broken
I received
conflicting information
later the levees
information
only topped
because

After
the neighbor
and his raft
we wade.

We spend
the next night
in an abandoned bus.

Pink plastic curler
safety pin
toothbrush nested
in sweating mud.
What longs for hair
for teeth for tether.

We are only bodies

bodies exhaust in moments

return in increments
of light's
slow rise.

Where the Current Takes

terrafirma

current anchored to my body

alarm clock :: pen :: chair :: desk :: computer :: water filter
shower curtain :: razor :: comb :: toothbrush :: hanger

current of the human body

and the task becomes impossible did I say gone –
no: chemically engineered durability no:
glacial rate of biodegradation

us

a current leads out of the human body
and back into lymph nodes eventually
my breast beginning age 11

unsinkable

I just want to say one word to you just one word

yes sir

are you listening

yes I am

plastics

exactly how do you mean

there's a great future in plastics think about it will you think about it

yes I will

entanglement of marine fauna ingestion by seabirds and organisms
ranging in size from plankton to marine mammals dispersal of microbial
and colonizing species to potentially nonnative waters concentration and
transport of organic contaminants to marine organisms

matter

the trail   intricate anger blooming just about then   to say —

creature

who knows what's down there down there deep so deep and dark
   the fish have no eyes –
what else lives down there like aliens breathing in the water

20

I cannot stand an aquarium the lantern fish and squid give me the
    creeps the beluga swims
round and round and round and round and round and round and
    round and round

rise
in the surface velocity field created by wind-driven Ekman currents
and geostrophic circulation this convergence zone indicated by
converging streamlines extends across most of the subtropical
North Atlantic basin and coincides with the highest observed plastic
concentrations –

the current leads out of the body –

as children we sent paper boats down the ravine creek
and followed them all the way to the sewage drain
came back with red welts nettle stings at ankles and calves
hurt more than they itched; later itched more than they hurt

The Water in You

Slippery folds of the largest
body and its needs.
I in the seams of your skin.

Eighty-three percent of blood –
deepest water. Transference.

The tap runs hot, gushes
from somewhere
very far away.

The condition of having a body
turned into itself.

Every night, drain. Suds spin away
under tile; the pipe
elbow-bends to treatment.

All wet within. Surface tension,
bubbled lung.

Blackwater froth freezes
against concrete walls in holding
tank to tank until clear.

Blood carries metabolic waste to your exhale –
cold night air smoked by breath, condensed release.

I under your nails I in the navel cup
I grime in all the places
the world enters your body.

Boundary Line

Mississippi heaves; Lewis and Clark drown.
The river eddies its tongue across their bronze chests,
licks Clark's cleft chin, swallows the tip of an elbow.
The hot gleam of gateway under the Saint Louis arch –

> *all this I carry and all this I ferry and my banks are mud and my banks*
> *are mud and I shine only what the sky gives me your children will come*

east, the water drags reflected sky: a surprised blue
between spindly, spit-off trees. Graveyard to the west –
row after lozenged row of hoods popped open,
gapings where engines once hummed –

> *to my banks of mud and your name not on my tongue and your name not*
> *on their tongues I swallow the stars and I eat your tears and I have all*
> *these years*

north, fumes of water treatment and a white plaque to mark
where nine people once set on the midnight river, sailed
that invisible line: Missouri slave, Illinois free.
But neither sheriff nor merchant were men
to lose so easy. They waited –

carried this body this body this bank loosened this mud I eat and
I will never and you will never some future swallow and at the end of all
   this

the other shore, the May night so close
against their faces they might have drowned.
No one went under but pistols went off,
shackles on, and bodies dragged back. Whippings
to blood and a mother sold downriver –

   a gulf and at the end of all this a body so warm I lose myself
   in tributary your name as salt this salt a gull a gully a gull a gully

Says City Water

ballast to basin a-splash from Catskills and go –

southward city bound :: duck through the aqueduct

through bedrock and fast :: water tunnel number one

water tunnel number two fluoride and floc

I am pure blue flow hello :: pressure

all the way up to any sixth floor

I've got the force fist-full you need me this way

I'm underground :: listen on your morning walk

your subway ride :: listen to the quickening below

hello to Delaware rush Croton rush

all the skinny pipes we travel through

freak force of push :: once we were without

containment now you feel me against

your shoulder sweet spot flesh

fall on feather far-off mountain I remember

branch tip and humus trickle :: when

the reservoir dissolved I effaced

deep through the underground systems

carry me carry me home girl carry me

home into your body :: rush tap and filter

spume of faucet :: my drip drip into your tub

your sink your belly basin

NY Harbor Waters to Manatee, October

winter's just about here I feel the cool against surfaced maw ::
yours :: and the muck below slows – hear it? chatterbox crabs
burrowing...

go south creature you're headed wrong

Mannahatta's long gone no more beavers slap-dashering any more
:: gone and gone :: they do alter like that take you to the brink and
– your boat-scarred face and – sure flames never burst my back
like the Cuyahoga out west I mean water catching fire imagine that
buddy! but still I stank all that clutter at my gut listen –

what heart here is manned? what harbor's ever a place? no pity for
this whole stupid crew

listen the warmth you loll in is fakery sham falsey runoff from the
refinery soon I'll crack at the edges slough-slough of shoreline ice
you've never heard such a sound before and I'll kill you before you
do that lettuce they dump in to sop up their guilt won't feed you
long enough I'm telling you :: the fact of wind and how it cuts their
skin and they retreat...

sure you've gone farther north than this the blue blue up there
filters summer sun sugar but change comes fast :: what's wrong with
your warm home shallows and frond floats and that balmy light at
your back?

adventure over kid you may be a face but from here on out it's all
propeller :: all propeller no skin

When All

Now the bumblebees and now the white-nosed bats.
All the colors. The disappeared frogs
line up in terrible splendor.

Take water – how it bends
to earth's curve or spills
across a table and evaporates: disappears!
Or a wheezing boy on his red bicycle,
and a rumble and sprung garbage truck.

    I lay my palm out.

    All the lines converge.

DEAR DISAPPEARING

…where do we begin and where do we end?
At our skin? Or as far as we can see?
…What sort of place is my body?
…what is the body a place for?

— Malin Hedlin Hayden on the work of Antony Gormley

Wave rolling to shore once background
now foreground :: split accented light.
The world outside the body never contained.

Be not contained.
Animal that lips the shoreline :: edge of our open mouth.
Impossible utterance.

Utter loss? Forget impossible
dear disappearing :: *goodbye* cannot fill the ocean.
Our ridiculous bodies tremble. And still

the wind drops and
alluvium collects :: the end of winter cannot mend
our interrupted selves.

What to cling to
:: no thought in the light
:: no light in the narrows.

The sound :: we have kept
this opening to ourselves :: have held it close.
Waiting to become

rust and salt and barnacled ::

stillness

a legibility we pass through.

———

Dear disappearing,

When you go where do you go?

> *Into the sea bed into the deep,*
> *into the ground, the long wet fleet.*

To whom do we say our rusty prayers?

> *To perch keeping watch over lead*
> *and ledger. To egret and frog, to bees.*

What will save us from our own splintering?

> *You many on your crowded log, lean*
> *in and scoop, scoop the scum water clean.*

And when our arms grow heavy as mercury?

> *The tree, the tree, the very last tree.*
> *Watch its leaves shake to the dirty-ditty breeze.*

Heat at winter's edge
and the desert floods
:: all the world gone topsy.

I give you cause
you give back loss
the way spring's snow crust

surrenders under a body's weight.
Still. Wide sky,
a blue you could sing to ::

one bird :: brown and incidental :: lifts in the wind.
Pleasure.
We cannot create

more than this
:: the place at the other
side of appearance.

We begin
whole. We corrode.
Stay on the tongue

:: but now it is a far off

wave and what the sunlight tricks

and what the body tricks :: we are all seeing what we wish.

———————

Matter transforms human
body to maggot nest the hiss
of dry ice against a metal sink.

Flesh shreds or just grows old
and turns to dirt to concrete to building
:: internal energy equals heat minus work.

Wood to smoke becomes
a manifestation of something else
:: smell that lingers a tenuous

cling to my jacket's cotton lining.
If burning is not disappearing
then neither is drowning :: the body

shows up again on another shore
in the folds of a current
whisked through the Atlantic.

Translation is a form
of disappearance :: my name gone
all wrong in their mouths.

Desire is not disappearing
:: desire is the other side :: desire
makes appearing come upon us.

The tankers are not disappearing
full symbols of loss.
But disappearing is not always so.

:: When you go, where do you go? ::

Flush against the sky a human
silhouette on a building's ledge.
Return utterance to form.

My mouth shapes sounds strung together
I have been contradicted before
:: my body discounted in the war of many meanings.

———

Dear disappearing,

What is the rank and what is the given?

> *The beast is but you and your merited skin,*
> *teller of nothing, farewell worn thin.*

In tune and in tremor, what do we gain?

> *The body a body like all other needs.*
> *You'll gawk and you'll follow the maze of the bees.*

And what if our buildings are simply too late?

> *You'll unbury treasure, you'll learn unlearn speech,*
> *your body, bodily wakes from its sleep.*

And what of redemption; what flashes the sky?

> *Not tulip nor heron; no wait for illusion –*
> *the knob of the earth, the human allusion.*

⁓

The spill
:: sea thick in welter.
What cracks?

Rush and form.
No salt to place
in anyone's mouth.

———

Frankly trouble. And then –
oh to be elliptical to be the planet's path.

I have watched them go round and round and
wish to never descend. Descent a fact of gravity

burst a fact of pressure. They upend they preen
enumerate what spills :: crude blow flow.

Extract meaning from _____
:: who turns around and says what happened

was delirium? Or censure. Says
what happened never did. Dare you.

We've got birds singing at two a.m. in the uplit sky.
Forget circadian rhythms :: rocked off the _____

They'll crack open the ocean yet the day not yet
:: see how we do? Girdle and lift? Don't mind

the pictures :: feathers oil-soaked. We'll always suffer
the right time for a lotion-covered tissue.

What is your balm made of, dear skin-soft-as-a-baby's—
Done with your sniffling? Upandatem!

There's a pile of _____ to be washed
and that blue detergent sure does wonder.

————

Sure the best country this once and always was.
The best one the worst it's just a technical matter

definition clarification. Let us try :: did we not build
the bomb the big one the one to end all ones?

They watch while we wilt and flourish wilt and flourish
then grow a third eye. What miracle what curlicue.

It's true we don't follow plans thought-out or otherwise.
It's the joy of improvisation good people. We take to the
    clink-a-clink

grow bold until treatment erodes and who _____
:: no one can judge or make us retrospect.

We spectacle.
We devour image clean and quick as candy.

———

They say the pleasure is the image. You trust?
The smile that fences cash. The glib that seals the oil anguish,

the soft-shoe shore recovery that moving-picture fancy.
Hear the clink-a-clink-a-piece? We tell them

:: keep it coming cowboy. Keep the club
white and manned. Keep it all from showing

its crackup into disaster :: as if they could
:: as if what comes around. Here's how we do

:: dig deep into. They excavate we'll dance.
When they find more than we see we'll clink-a-clink-a-

trouble. No, we'll be more than trouble we'll be terra-siren
jackrabbit caterwaul cassandra cassandra :: we'll be worth it all.

———

Children of pleasure we make and take we spectate.
Jelly-jar history :: this wave and wave

of capital-A landscape. See it cinescope into undeniable desire
:: that soaring cliff :: dawn's endless sky :: roiling orgasmic waters
   shot ecstatic.

Yes! Our claim our geography our ever-always
optimism quivering in every blade of prairie grass

every pine needle each boulder so solid we make and are made
:: here this land :: made out as if blank-slated and ripe for the
   plucking.

Greedy our fingers thorn-scarred and still hungry.
(Here's how we come undone :: _____)

Rainbow sheen across aquatic field.

Start up the engine :: key in slot :: spark :: ignition

:: its chuff chuff grin to say how we're so worth it.

If it spills we disperse if it leaks they kill if we deadzone

they optimize the clink-a-clink-a-cash. Watch us flame always and
   evermore –

they litigate to thin and then horizons :: by dint and by jolly jolly
   treasure.

I've been in line to stand for person ::

for such a long time and now

the shop's shuttered and no other thing's awake.

Someone near me asked, "Who united the war?"

Someone else said, "A lost felt."

Can't escape the head all those neurons shuttling thought.

See everyone behaves or seems to

like "it's not their problem."

I have to admit infuriation. What's this I'm breathing?

But here. *Body*, our bright, metered field.

Drape me

in barnacles and salt :: watch me turn marvelous.

In my body the skin leaves without farewell
the hair without farewell
the blood pricks pain farewell.

The muck of the afternoon,
all rain and mud,
brings the outside in.

And the man dead for days
in the apartment above me
has finally disappeared :: taken away.

Trouble with the resounding wings
of the fly :: who knows where it has landed
before. Decomposing flesh :: what rots.

Transference of tissue is not disappearing.
And when does the system fail?
I open my purse to nothing but stale air.

———

Dear disappearing,

Why score the space if the blank is a site of action?

> *What looks like nothing surges*
> *a field of vast, invisible choreography.*

What if you caught up with us?

> *We'd mouthful the same,*
> *always charging forward.*

A revelation or a trick?

> *The meaning muddles*
> *in the faint image trace.*

———

The question does not disappear.
Indifferent landscape. The last glacier
at the equator melts, streams

away in the soaking rain.
Rushing water :: the sound
of no goodbye

:: the disappearing moment
becomes
its own ascent.

Dear disappearing,

What is this slow disintegration?

>*Rust and a melting away.*
>*The chemistry of disappearance.*

And the mud that stiffens into clay?

>*Does not disappear.*
>*Simply transforms.*

All this time I've been trying to make you turn around, to see what features gangle.

>*The retina exists to record image – everything after that's electric*
>*pulse. Biology. Magic rendered.*

And still I'm a flimsy string, thrum and thrumming at your translucent back.

>*Here. Crawl up the skeleton loop – our shoulder blades,*
>*these tiny wings bent.*

How long until we go?
 Water and its immense weight,
:: like image and its pleasure

:: dearly dearly we covet
the tender sea
not yet ripped out :: the weed.

Molecules tend so close
to each other.
Open your palms.

We need more
than the saturated element
more than a shoulder tilted

to the wind turbines. Hush
and we listen to that gorgeous
chest heartbeating ocean.

TENACIOUS AS SALT

The Seasons and Their Tremendous Rules Are Breaking

The window is open because summer can't quite leave.
I have a firm attachment to the progression of a year
and to her delicate body. I'm watching our bellies float

an inch above the mattress. The seasons are uncoupling
meaning from sensation, so I am not asleep.
Where do I look for order? In the way

the Web defines fact – memes, porn, apps?
When she and I step into the world's vast rules,
we refute anomalous mirrors. Ever so natural

gender. Disrupt, play. Still, we are unsettled
by increasing manifestations of change in the atmosphere.
There are so many words that might define

the way we course over terrain of water, weather
skin, and bed sheet. A mesmerizing, inchoate ride.
Later, I ask if I can meander along her tidy festoon.

As if such borders existed between us.
The concept of *sweater* growing faint
and resplendent as the year wears on.

Continuity

On the boardwalk my gilled woman laughs. *Don't be blue, don't be blue.*
True or false: how and what disappears? Was the time
going on, were the waves crash and uncrashing along

what shoreline? I admit to being thrilled
by ocean's particles. She says, "Salt in mouth." You bicycle, you plastic
thing. *We girls are very good at getting what we want.*

Once, we communicated like occasional rain: unpredictable,
brief, humid. My glasses make a form for translation. If we could
understand, finally, each other's language, we'd near

something transparent on this fraught journey. You say, "Baby, come
and take a ride in my bowl full of blueberries." Afraid
of getting old-lady knees, we remain nevertheless full believers

in mini-skirts. You want motion to be the same as thinking.
I don't know if thinking is the same as feeling, but emotion's impulse
could be the brain's delivery of order: body switches codes,

becomes the mind's vocabulary. An intermediary?
As if militant? You take off your shoes for freedom. There are other
ways of solving conflicts. Words, for instance. *Be a good one*

that way. Be a good one that way. And so gender becomes
an object. You want a looseness that makes me
nervous. I want to become the woman your parents

never dreamed for you. The buildings in long rows, blank windows
giving off a smell of domesticity. We consider desire seriously.
I could tell a lie, *but in the end the lie tells me.*

Sea Change

now water becomes tangible to tooth
and gives all :: full-weather assault
and we are not boundless ::

                    nest, egg, a flutter of a plastic bag ::
the children haven't even hatched

and I'm thinking of blood, heavier than water,
a mess of desire :: impulse ::
    a child will say a name
and that name will become my body ::
no covering of fabric or image

the world enters our room through
the sentimental forgetfulness of building materials
:: no please or thank you when it comes to winter ::
even the overheating radiator is no match for this resolve

I'm wanting to burrow down and ask for a kind of forgiveness

there are parts of what I must call *my heart*
that I can only touch at times ::
unpredictable slide from one scale to the next

like now, I want to return

to the problem of the white plastic in the kites' nest :: bully

:: strongest bird :: surviving egg ::

                                   we let go what we create

:: detritus :: our restless imaginations ::

but I take more than I give up

:: I've met very little without protection,

without a little bit of defense ::

now I'm raw :: holding nothing across my chest

Shutoff

When the tap no longer runs at the flick of a wrist,
no flush and the bathroom mirror shimmers cold
we knock around like dried bones,
the kettle empty, dinner dishes crusting in the sink.
It depends not on the wheels that spin above
but our subterranean veins, monstrous capillary system
exposed in the pit scooped open streetside.
Gape at the laying bare, crossed and dirt-clung pipes
that deliver us our daily gas and water. Unearthed
for a fix, the mechanicals, the failings.
Our life turns over like a little engine. We open
and desire rushes out and out to run clear.
A million little lives turn over, a million gallons gush,

bluewhite glaciers nudge and push out to sea.

A Kind of Molting

On the first warm day of spring there's wind
and pollen and without my overcoat
I'm a few pounds lighter walking from one end
of the city to the other. That's some kind of freedom.

Like the time I tried to construct
a bed for you but realized we needed a boat
just longer than our legs. Now's about
a good time to set sail.

It's easy to forget we live
on an island until a strong wind
brings the salt water to certain
neighborhoods. Just like it's easy

to forget our parents are aging, too,
until their bones are replaced
by metal parts, pins,
and resistance under stapled skin.

Mom learns to walk again
and we learn what it means to hold a shoulder firm
what it means to live in a city so fragile at its edges
disintegration and inundation remain distinct possibilities,

and no number of flashlights,
no amount of sand or love can keep
what happens from happening. Until now
we were misled by water towers,

those round-bellied gods on roofs giving us false
promises of a drink without end.

Flickering Towards Definition

when the light hits the crosswalk ::
rain soaked :: there's a dog-not-dog :: its definition
a no-where :: there was a where

and there was a here :: Manhattan on a cold spring
night :: wolf at the crosswalk a wild no-
where its coat of light and rain on asphalt shining

off a ways the train makes its station over the bridge
:: our icons gone fractal the way light circularizes
scratches on perception's steel facade :: I think

my body is a linguist's best intention :: last-
minute agency :: I relax when your words
daisy chain your "here" to mine…

are we a ton of explanation? you could
reference Deleuze and Guattari if you prefer :: inevitable
code switch and language's weighted privilege

:: still there's the no-dog at the very real
crosswalk and its slow saunter to the other side
knocking over pedestrians :: you could insert

a Marxist reference here :: but no one's around to say much
until we – it, you, me – are the only ones left standing,
our tongues elaborately tied bows, our skin wet with city drizzle

When the Weather Quits You

The church, at the off-hour, rings
its bells. They stop
before the tune's resolution.

Rain, a strange sister.

All day, we walk
around feeling
some absence we cannot place.

———

Umbrellas splay some absence we cannot place. I do not open all day.
Feeling your mouth before the tune's resolution, a slim crescent of an
otherwise whole. When the weather turns, bells on the ground. The
penumbra scatters the off-hour: I walk. Rain, a strange sister.

———

I talked all morning
without mentioning specifics, without
uttering them at all.

During the partial eclipse, I stared
at the ground, the penumbra
scattering slim crescents.

Your mouth.

I do not open.

The umbrella splays.

What We've Left to Shore

When the fortune teller said,
"Search the singing machine,"
she meant we'd one day find

our voices hidden
in a box with gears.
An ever-present hum

at the base of the city, undercurrent.
to everyone's sleep,
soundtrack to our somnambulism.

"Bring the oil," I said, "bring the charge,
one zero, one one,
one socket."

It's not us, it's the legacy
of our bones. This tilting to the earth.
And what if we move

to the place outside our skin,

pretend a garden, a sun,

pretend a pastoral house?

Where Water Falls Off the Horizon

To wake the cistern,
drop a stone and
listen for its splash.

If a dull thud,
it is too late.

The blue tarp,
edges all thread,
flaps its corner
in the wind.

———

Magnificent balloon.

Self removed from body
tethered by a string.

Magnificent buffoon.

The wind does what it pleases.
Reach for me at arm's length.

———

Fast water. I cannot see
below the surface.
There must be trout, pebbles,
heavy metals, microbes.

What eats the waste eats the pleasure.

The moss furred
on the boulder so green
it shouts.

The Rainy Season

Loosens mud.
Now, it's all sex –
green heads, buds,
the spider trembling
in her web.

You pull your bright red thread.
I hear the tiny bird
call out its slim territory:
sediment, sediment, sediment.

Sweet, the river
rolls and rolls,
such skin
for the thorn-bush grows.

When we whip
like this in wind
our bodies' kite thrills.
Quick – pin tight
the double knot,
recite the alphabet

and climb up
the diamond tree –

it's all panorama
and bark-scraped knees,
love, from here on out.

Water East

East River

Over and under a thousand times, my body travelling across filigreed bridges named for the boroughs on the banks, through the tunnels kept from flood by the constant sump pumps. From Brooklyn's shimmy to Manhattan's rage, from Manhattan's swan to Brooklyn's fur, and back and back again. Our bodies at the Brooklyn shore the summer you and I – Whitman's others *ever so many hundred years hence* – kissed the rhythm of the tidal strait, the flood tide and ebb tide.

Love what always changes –
river, its fickle back casting
sky's each light.

Miles below, the subway curves in screech and hurtle, my body rattles under pressure. I look at people's faces. Kin, but no one gives away our private intimacies. Amassed, crowded into the dank, we are here because we came and never left. One bend into the next and we rise up and out, a new layer of sediment across our bodies. Riverbed and clay, what we all once were.

Wellfleet

Land arches into the Atlantic, curved finger. The wind, so fierce on
the east shore, dies to something like a hum on the west shore. The
path ends at muddy beach grass, a tiny inlet dictated by tides. Once
a carcass – huge fish or small shark – stank up the whole shore. We
go in May, pack jackets and hats we've already discarded in the city.
Clean sky, the sun angling sharp into the water. We watch crabs
make sand balls, place them carefully next to each other with their
one small claw, one big.

Leaving, we crush
tiny spiral patterns –
sand into sand.

We go on like this in contentment and the tide goes out in the
morning. With you asleep, I walk out to the fresh, bare flats. The
mud pulls at my boots. I cannot move without sinking. I suck in my
breath. A mile from the grassed edge of land, no phone. How will
you find me? I lift my panicked foot. This time, the mud lets go. I
pick my way back to you. At the hose I wash muck from my boots
stinking of seaweed, fortune, salt.

Hudson River

If we take the train and the river widens to our left – winter-black,
white curled caps, the Palisade cliff face and bare trees in bone
wind. If we pass the bridge, the fort, plumes from the plant. If the
water travels north with us, if at the same time it runs south, for
fifty miles mixed like this – salt pushing up, snow melt pushing
down to the harbor to bed the ocean tide. If we hike the mountain,
if we stop for the etched view: the five-street town, the country
road, and the train's trail along the riverbank.

When we exhale
the water in our lungs transforms.
Singular breath, wood smoke.

Then in such field quiet we understand our alliance to that
bay down south crowded with ghost ships and torch, elbowed
skyscrapers, underground velocity, to our own chaotic bodies that
have followed us north, tenacious as salt's press.

Talking into Each Other's Mouths

You say, "If the Cumbre Vieja volcano erupts,
half the island of La Palma will plunge into the sea and then…"

>Rise up, Atlantic! Find us wanting at the harbor's mouth,
>Coney Island lingers a mermaid's lemonade
>before the irrevocable tear, the bridges tossed sticks,
>Prospect just a phrase on the tip, and O!
>Whitman and his houses tumble into the pull,
>names gone dumb –

"…but some people doubt the mega-tsunami theory,"
you say, glancing up from your screen.

>Out the window, the trees' bare branches
>undulate like seaweed. "See the current," I say,
>"our street signs fall, the houses lose their bricks."

You spread your arms. Draw up the sail, sweetheart.
Our room's a tight box ship. We billowy milk and wet paper
take the hit and spindrift. We wave and wave and wave.

Notes

"Look Alive, Dark Side"

Italicized phrase from Greg Delory, a researcher at the University of California at Berkeley, commenting on the discovery of water on the moon in 2009.

John Johnson Jr.. "'The moon is alive,' NASA says after water discovery," *LA Times* (November 14, 2009): accessed November 11, 2012, http://www.latimes.com/news/nationworld/nation/la-sci-moon14-2009nov14,0,2036369.story.

"Wade"

Italicized lines from testimony by Michael Brown, former director of Federal Emergency Management Agency (FEMA), during post-Katrina congressional hearings.

"Former FEMA Director Testifies Before Congress," *The New York Times* (September 27, 2005): accessed November 11, 2012, http://www.nytimes.com/2005/09/27/national/nationalspecial/27text-brown.html?pagewanted=print&_r=0.

"Where the Current Takes"

Source text in sections titled "unsinkable" and "rise":

"*The Graduate* 'One Word: Plastics'," YouTube video, 0:58, from *The Graduate*, directed by Mike Nichols, (Embassy Pictures Corporation, 1967), posted by "Lance Ehlers," November 9, 2007, http://www.youtube.com/watch?v=PSxihhBzCjk.

Kara Lavender Law, Skye Morét-Ferguson, Nikolai A. Maximenko, Giora Proskurowski, Emily E. Peacock, Jan Hafner, and Christopher M. Reddy, "Plastic accumulation in the North Atlantic subtropical gyre," *Science* 329, no. 5996 (2010): 1185.

"Dear Disappearing"
    Gormely's project, "Another Place," placed a hundred solid
    cast iron body forms (of Gormley's own body) along the coast
    of the Kugelbake in Germany. The statues – now permanently
    installed at Crosby Beach in the UK – all face the horizon. From
    Gormley's website: "The idea was to test time and tide, stillness
    and movement, and somehow engage with the daily life of the
    beach. This was no exercise in romantic escapism. The estuary of
    the Elbe can take up to 500 ships a day and the horizon was often
    busy with large container ships."

    "Another Place, 1997": accessed November 11, 2012, http://www.antonygormley.
    com/sculpture/item-view/id/230#p0.

    The phrase "the place at the other side of appearance," page 37,
    is Gormley's own.

    "Antony Gormley": accessed November 11, 2012, http://en.wikipedia.org/wiki/
    Antony_Gormley.

    All text on page 43 sourced from *Moby-Dick*.

    Herman Melville, *Moby-Dick* (New York: Bantam Dell, 2003).

"Flickering Towards Definition"
    The phrase "there was a where and there was a here" by Cecilia
    Viacuña.

    Cecilia Viacuña (lecture, Flux Poetics, Dixon Place, NY, April 19, 2011).

"Water East"

Italicized phrase in the section titled "East River" is Walt Whitman's.

Walt Whitman, "Crossing the Brooklyn Ferry," *Leaves of Grass and Selected Prose*, ed. Lawrence Buell (New York: Random House, 1981), 125-133.

Recent Titles from Alice James Books

Alice James Books has been publishing poetry since 1973 and remains one of the few presses in the country that is run collectively. The cooperative selects manuscripts for publication primarily through regional and national annual competitions. Authors who win a Kinereth Gensler Award become active members of the cooperative board and participate in the editorial decisions of the press. The press, which historically has placed an emphasis on publishing women poets, was named for Alice James, sister of William and Henry, whose fine journal and gift for writing went unrecognized during her lifetime.

Designed by Pamela A. Consolazio
LITTLE FROG DESIGNS

Printed by Thompson-Shore
on 30% postconsumer recycled paper
processed chlorine-free